American Lit

poems by

Jacob Minasian

Finishing Line Press
Georgetown, Kentucky

American Lit

Copyright © 2020 by Jacob Minasian
ISBN 978-1-64662-123-1 First Edition
All rights reserved under International and Pan-American Copyright Conventions. No part of this book may be reproduced in any manner whatsoever without written permission from the publisher, except in the case of brief quotations embodied in critical articles and reviews.

ACKNOWLEDGMENTS

"Empty" first appeared in *Linden Avenue Literary Journal*
"American Pasture" first appeared in *Museum of Americana*
"Voyage to Emily Dickinson's Grave" was first published in *Carbon Culture Review* as "Voyage to a Graveyard"
"Meta" first appeared in *Causeway Lit*
"Convo with Abe" first appeared in the 40th Anniversary Edition of *RipRap Literary Journal*
"Placebo Opus" was first published as "Just Stop" in *Gyroscope Review*
"Wine Country" was published by the Academy of American Poets on Poets.org and *Fire and Rain: Ecopoetry of California* by Scarlet Tanager Books

My deepest gratitude goes out to the people who helped encourage, advise, and inspire me during the creation of these poems: Brenda Hillman, Matthew Zapruder, Geoffrey G. O'Brien, Cedar Sigo, Marilyn Abildskov, Rickey Laurentiis, Brett Fletcher Lauer, Matthew Schmidt, Patrick Howell, and my fellow students during my time in the Saint Mary's College of California MFA Program in Creative Writing. Also, to the amazing writers, faculty, and staff at the Leopardi Writing Conference, and the Juniper Summer Writing Institute.

And, of course, to my family, for their fueling love and support.

Publisher: Leah Maines
Editor: Christen Kincaid
Cover Art: Jacob Minasian
Author Photo: Helena Minasian
Cover Design: Elizabeth Maines McCleavy

Printed in the USA on acid-free paper.
Order online: www.finishinglinepress.com
    also available on amazon.com

Author inquiries and mail orders:
Finishing Line Press
P. O. Box 1626
Georgetown, Kentucky 40324
U. S. A.

Table of Contents

Empty 1

American Pasture 2

Stopwatch 3

Communion 5

Twentieth of March 7

Memory Loss 8

From a Bridge 9

Voyage to Emily Dickinson's Grave 10

Hearth 12

Meta 13

Convo with Abe 14

Campaign 15

American Lit 16

Placebo Opus 24

Wine Country 28

For my parents

and for Helena

Empty

At the glowing entrance
to the Meijer, a woman
stops at the 25 cent
toy vending machines,
small plastic and rubber
trinkets, as if she is
shopping, face without
expression, her cart carrying
bread and eggs. I walk past her
through the entrance vestibule and
past the welcomer staring blankly
away from anything reminiscent
of any thing. In my refrigerator,
on a cocktail sauce jar, a crust
sits between rim and lid.
A fortune cookie I open two
days too late is missing its fortune.

American Pasture

On the side of the 42,
a valley cuts into trees
to home telephone poles.
Further, swollen brick
houses, their elaborate
lawns, are undivided by
fences, though concealed
carry seems to draw
them closed, I'm sure,
by gun property sight lines.
On one of the lawns, an
afraid Native American
caricature is a bad statue
with hands posed
high above an inaccurate
headdress, an American
flag stabbed in the grass
next to him. I try
not to lose focus on the
road - a box that, if
you leave, you might die.
I stop by the Meijer,
and pass a small boy yelling
yee-haw as he waves on a
mechanical horse, while
his mother tries to split
a nickel into a childhood.

Stopwatch

Everything is waiting

                        to fall. Names not yet
on the coroner's lips,

      or in digital ink, tagged
                              with a sad thumbs-up.

               We umbrella against incorrect

    emails from a held office,
                      may not have

    chosen our president,

the investigation, a movie
                            waiting to be shot

    in some future
       year, no

                   matter the eventuality.
Waiting for panic, a
        faux alarm
              to Hawaii, and now
                      waiting for when

                the ballistic missiles are real.

Take immediate cover, don't
        wait, this is not exercise.
                People begot between these
                      borders watch
            their parents plucked like
      petals in the grass-
   fires swallowing
                the coastline, cold storm
                        fronts used as propagandizing
      proof that the planet isn't
what it is. Floods dragging
our lacking through
                   California streets. The
        torrid mountain on
             newsfeed streams burns

                    the closest to imagining hell.
      People buy Napa Valley
wine when they see collapsed
                markets. An electronic
     road sign says an adult is
             missing, and gives the city,
      and plate numbers,
on an Ohio highway.

Communion

Punctured freeways bend
around late February,
its empty Ohio branches,
water jumping off
the road onto the bones
under the back of my
hand hanging
out the automatic
window. A train
is a rusted postcard
with its red clay and
white, gray steel rivets,
refineries depositing cloud
against cloud, odd out-
of-place superimposition.
Neighborhoods appear
colder from their unsupported
mortar and brick. Traffic layers
from an overturned truck,
red blue lights reflected in
eyes, reflected
in side mirrors, which
render at a bit farther distance.
I try not to hold on to the unjust
honks in my direction. Horns
twitter like audio glitter across
car hoods. A hawk
stilts the sky its dazzling
wingspan. The freeway levels
to a plateau, over-
looking the metal wasteland,
plumes rising from the stacks
like some brutal aftermath.

The nearer we draw to the boiling
coffee behind counters,
the more the un-focused
thoughts arrive
from perceived stillness.
Everything is
fighting at the molecular
degree. Concrete
becomes a jam. The ology
of formation. My phone screen
doesn't react to a tap,
and for a sharp second
I wonder where my
life has gone.

Twentieth of March

The equinox will end with a snow
storm, eighty percent by ten
in the evening at thirty seven
degrees. Through the night
it will continue to deconstruct
specific colors, all into one,
and by eleven the next
morning there will be
feet to march through.
Even now, the gray
squirrels disappear, the
geese are abruptly gone.
Roots scramble
around their trunks
like some warming
self-embrace against
the ever-dropping air.
Institutions will close,
postponing, perhaps
preventing tragedy
similar to the one
in the news today.

Memory Loss

At first, it's a quick ditch,
money and tweeted sorrow.
A chance for analysts
to turn equations, popular
monsters to quote psychiatry,
turn red into green
into red states and open carry,
as if everyone is safe with
more automatic machine rifles
that can bury hundreds
by the minute. As if
we should all have
hot hips ready to roast powder,
all have the power to
nuke a meadow.
Next, it's piling dirt on top.

From a Bridge

The river's toxic
affix is hidden in
height's distance.
I stare past the metal fence,
bent like a web,
to the soap factories, how
they match the crimson
brick at the corner
of a porch I don't
remember in California,
a shade darker than
the quotidian plant pot,
whose fate I can now
only picture in the
optimism of soil.
The snow has
lasted late into March.
The tracks empty
their broken
grins into the train yard.
Robins, with their bright
bronze chests, seem
to be the only
ones who know
they're part superhero.

Voyage to Emily Dickinson's Grave

Two people take their seats by
windows they're afraid to look out
during takeoff, when pressure
in the ears fluctuates
conversations about who will
pull the exit handle in a possible
plummet, something like
*you're tall, so you reach
across me* or you get
the picture amidst the
prayers and screaming
turbines, which could
be by now smoking
over the elaborate
distant broccoli of
forest, breaking only
for the sail speckled
surface light on
water's cutting
similar shape to the
woman's profile sitting
beside me with closed
eyes and strung out
knuckles over the
shared arm
rest, far into being over
Connecticut, and my
right shoulder has
hurt for weeks, though
I am afraid to graze
the woman afraid to look
out the window during
takeoff, whose pen
inks her hands as she
marks in a leather dark
blue book over Connecticut,

now, with the water and
forest below, layered
in movement as the tree
I'll see, chewing gum hours
after, sore to the jaw,
I land and sit looking
through a window at
light on leaves, wind rolling
branches, the bright and dark
green shuffling
a silent applause, hours
before I'll stand at the tombstone
of a poet in Amherst, and run
fingertips across marble, and
lift my face to the boundary
of sun and shade, not far
from faded brick, a dock,
a mirror, a coast
opposite a coast where
a patch plugs the sea,
a meaning constructed through
breath, greased hands plugging
away at plugging into raw
fuel veins under the surface
under the surface, off the coast
opposite the coast miles from
my half-shadow in a cemetery, though I am
still thinking on a plane over water and
roots, or maybe the other way.

Hearth (After Giorgio de Chirico's "The Philosopher's Conquest")

Artichokes, you are my favorite
pizza topping. I'll take you
with me from this meaningless
corridor, to wait in this waiting
room blessedly devoid of current
events. No, they're
there, a patient with
a fuse lit out of sight, and
we can wonder together who
will be called first. I love
your hearts, artichokes, their
particular salt and wine,
the slight vinegar, mixes
so well with melted butter
on a teacup-less saucer. You
are comfort and your company
now makes the stopped clock
more palatable. I do not desire
you steamed or atop pizza. I
smell burning coal. Iron. And
our rage must be stomached as
two shadows talk in approaching
volume. We must be polite, art-
ichokes. We must not rock the
ship that is too close to the rocks,
just on the other side of some
ancient industry. You see, we've
been waiting for that which rolls
by now, like watching from
the side of a highway as
relatives blur in the
windows of a passing car,
becoming carbonized air.

Meta

In a grass
the fire flinches backwards,
inhaling its conclusion, as
wood lightens over ember, and
iron tracks peel from the plain,
de-rusted spikes jousting
from their holdings, hills that
freckle over with game, birds,
buffalo, herds, curds at
the campfire re-tinned,
roofed, metal-lidded.
Native souls reversed back
into un-bloodied bodies.

Convo with Abe

Abraham Lincoln and I are riding rapid transit.
He is sitting. I'm standing, holding on to
the greasy metal. Someone coughs on my
shoulder. The train is loud and full.
"Are you surprised at how far we've come?"
I shout. He doesn't look up from the iPad in
his lap. I think of what he must think,
today's news glowing brightly from his legs.
"You shitting me?" He whispers, yet somehow
his voice is louder than everything.

Campaign

How many deaths have been
watched from the backseat?
Eyes avoided that
close to a suicide?
You begin to see
patterns. 11.08 on
the previous gas pumper's
price tag. Your brain
rearranging the letters in
a word in a letter, to make a
palindrome. The complainers
complain about the complaints.
All the good monsters have failed us.
This means warm unwelcoming
square miles. Patchy yards. We're only
neighbors if you have the same caliber
rifle or higher. Be about your vitamins.
I think there's some C in that orange
soda. Please. Be president of everything
you can be. We need you.

American Lit

I want to write a novel
in a Starbucks while people
clamber for their pumpkin
lattes only available when
cold approaches on time's
thin horizon, a novel about
a man who, while leaving
work, hears a couple
talking about polls
and how their preferred
candidate is down in
votes though they think
still has a chance and this
man leaving work scoffs
into the autumn because
he thinks his
candidate has
the advantage. Though he'll
discover he should
have known some part
of his cornea
perceived the signs,
literally on the lawns,
and that cold flinch
in his irises that became
something he was
suddenly swimming in
was not something he
should have even if he
could half-way dismiss.
And some kind of screen
shatters between his
eyes and the world and
everything is filtered
through an absent frame.

His apartment is
no longer his apartment,
adjoining rooms in which
in the
following months he will
watch the dismantling of
decency, and watch the earth
burn and freeze and flush
and swallow, and animals,
the animals, they
are tragedy's real forecast,
the snakes and vermin
that fled Vesuvius and
flooded the chariot-ground
streets of Pompeii, as the
man will watch earth-shaken
rivers flood the streets of
Southern California, as to
the north Napa lies scorched,
while east in Ohio, from where
the man watches, where summer
storms pummeled his windows,
now in these months, snow
storms last into spring, frozen
fronts blotching the Midwest
and the Atlantic coastline.
Winter, where it does not belong.
Like the gulf into Texas.

The days after the
election the man
at work gleans
each customer
the potential to be
party to the party

that blatantly shaped
such a destination.
And while a smoky
evening settles over
the 275, with
its bonfire air,
he listens to the
latest language lose
form into
puddles under
tongues, he takes a
mistaken turn, onto
a parallel road, past
sun-snowed meadows,
and there he
finds that he can
see right through the
trees, because the light
scales on indefinitely.
This moment later he
will think of as the office
scraps the land's
protections. The buffalo
of Yellowstone, the pelicans'
torpedo-like
dive into the Pacific's
silver bounty, the newt
braving its way through
floors of sequoias.
Muir Woods, Half Moon
Bay, the green on the shell
of the black crab with
red claws hiding
in the rocks along Stinson
Beach, the obsidian
serpent's shield-gridded skin,

Pantherophis alleghaniensis,
under the boulder near
Yellow Springs, Ohio,
the stone bridge above
all save sky
in Kentucky's Red River
Gorge, the everything
in vision, and that just
beneath it. The blue
heron's mirror in the fresh
inland water, the bullfrog
splayed in the vacation
cabin door-jam, the ears-flat
jaguar pacing San
Diego Zoo's display
container. The glass-globed
scorpion in an Arizona meteor
crater's gift shop. A pigeon
picking bread crumbs from
a bottle cap. Nuclear power
plants next to rivers
broken by fishhooks.
Lights like precious metal.

Soon he will split
time between processing
groceries and lecturing
under the sinking ceiling
of a college classroom.
One class in the old building,
the next two in the new.
One more would mean health
insurance and salary, which
etymologizes from *salarium*,

the value of salt, while
one full-time position
is retired for part-time,
and again it will happen,
and the man gives cheap
condolences for the
overpriced required
texts the spirit-store tolls
to the lined up students.

Now the man wakes
every morning he
tries to avoid
trying to avoid
the news, because
things are happening
like giving guns to teachers
to keep guns from
schools. Peaceful
protest pertains
to a color. And less
sense is quite clearly
playing the part of sensible.
A net that would rather
cough cash for a cell
than a treatment.
Words mean nothing.
He wants him to take
him at his word.

Periodically things
are pierced by art.

And one tuned blues-
pitch waters his eyes.

Shots fire the night
on a freeway where,
before, gun decals
line a car's rear window.

The deaths surpass
the grains of gun-
powder in the bullets
in an armory.

So this man tries to
write this in so many
poems about
the fall of brick
buildings, metaphor,
histories, anaphora.
Anaphora. Anaphora.
It all begins the same
way. Like snow
piling. Until he
can't even see the
lilacs in his mind.

A retired teacher takes
a double vodka next
to the central
character of my novel
on an airplane just to
talk about school boards
and psychiatry. This
system is sick in the
head, she says, and he
thinks to the day before
when he watched the value of

under oath being thrown aside
for official posturing. And
so the man sleeps each night
with birds in his mind,
haunted by that
moment the flock breaks
its beautiful direction.

The man lands in California
where the mountains are
even angrier.
He sits unknowingly
on the train in
a seat he had sat
in years before,
like it's the same
verse he somehow
echoes in toe taps.
The burrowing owls
no longer hold
up construction. The
windows them-
selves have changed.
One smoldering leaf
stars in the twilight.
Stores have
replaced air.

He thinks, anyone can look
around and see
what is happening.

There is whip cream on my coffee.
My phone is the same as the
person's sitting next to me,
which is the same as a computer,
which is the same as a human
looking into their palm.

I want to write a dystopian
novel about the
present though there's not
enough fiction.

Placebo Opus

Beginning the end of the cyclical cynical.
In the confidence continuum
our mirror becomes the brain
behind the eyes of the other person.
Hate for the body guillotines
the soul. Careful cartoon
coyote chasing dinner off
a cliff. You can't eat if you're dead.
You can't wear a swimsuit in your casket,
and a rotted tooth smile won't
make gaunt cheeks look so pretty.

Maybe if I say I'm not smart, or
I'm not cool and I'm so ugly,
maybe someone will argue with me,
and then I can believe them.
        Though

what if no one sticks up for the stuck down in the mud stick?
So you make a sign
and you wait, and you wear it around your neck,
though under your collar so no one can read it.

        Cut along the thigh
                where the tone should be.
        Cut along the arm
                so you wear long sleeves.
        Cut along the gut
                because it is not magazine
                      ready,
                      not magazine
                      ready.
                Knots of ready to
                      feel some pain
                      feel some pain,
                      feel something
        other than shame.

Stop with the bull-oney ornery ads agitating
our collective constitution, mindless mead feeding
the marrow-sucking soulless plane of tomorrow.
Just stop, I have no friends on Facebook, I just have
hundreds of people who are my friends on Facebook.
Stop. And if I post this heartbreak, I'll get bundles of "likes".
My mind has become a telegram reading of today. Stop.

Social media spreads the threads of synaptic conditioning,
so when it fires you fire, pull trigger, and click,
washing our eyes with contact constant through multiplied lenses.
Neurosis implants itself in young eyes growing in the screen world.
The (photo)bom-bardment of
       whoweshouldbe,
            whatweshouldwant,
                 howweshouldlook.
                     (And we send our friends the links.)

Hashtag hashtag hashtag,
       no wonder the hand pulls hair roots out from the scalp,
       roots out, burned land, out-rooted, like they'll take the
       "I can't take this" along with them.
       Let's get to the root, let's get to the route, let's get
       off of this circular driveway.

Beginning the end of the cyclical cynical.

Part t
          w
               o

I've seen beautiful humans voluntarily knifed
in an attempt to perfect what is already imperfectly perfect.
We're sorry, you've been disconnected from your body.
Please wake up and buy again.
Find the nearest wifi signal, the sky-high indulge
in this "why-try" impulse, but our eye's multilingual.
We don't look in one language. So why uniform our form?
Why saw the horn off the unicorn? There is a
mythology in all of us. Why un-tell that legend?

Interject an injection here, to mimic
wrinkle-free fabric, erasing the faces' character.
Add some angel to our skin through bacterial
toxicity, gifting paralysis to our muscles so our smiles
don't damage our dimples. Tox wrapped
in a Bo, commercializing cosmetic alteration,
hemming an identity dress. I can't change
the channel away from the trending towards
Chanel sunglass masks.
            I've seen enough and it's not even noon yet.

A fading vignette is the picture of today's synthetic superlative,
yet the flawed have far less flaws than the flawless.
Still, the sum would rather obscure into the mainstream marketing
glamour guzzle than suffer the illusion of living unnoticed lives.
It is the masses' manufactured marveling
          that will cause them to fade out of focus,
                         and disappear in the glitz.
          _____ ←This is them.

                              See the sparkles?

Let me spare suspense its 24-7 workload.
Your crazy is crazy, but society is mad bonkers insane.
Three hundred years ago it wasn't crazy
to burn innocent women on suspicion of witch-work,
                             (and sometimes we still do,
                                       with a different kind of fire.)
So if you think you're not make-it-to-tomorrow material, stop.
        If you think you're not not not together, stop.
And tell the sheep-shit-show-media-marketing-sewer-stew
                                       to stop.
                             To just stop.

Wine Country

History is written out of itself.
The Napa River spins, crosshatched
in the December wind. Scintilla
sitting on a timeline's shore. A blue
heron wings wide from its jutting
riverside roots. Sandpipers
feathering through puddled
mud. Loons dip their heads in
reflection, and the homes of swallows
stucco a bridge I pass underneath.
Barbeque and gelato line banks
where bars and jails arrived before,
living arranged so minorities
flooded first, down in a channel
now filled in to forget. Bright buildings
hide the hangman's rope. My kayak cuts
across surface. My oars source rings.
History is written out of itself.
A lichen rust on tree metal.

Jacob Minasian received his MFA from Saint Mary's College of California, where he was the 2016 Academy of American Poets University and College Poetry Prize winner. His work has appeared in publications including Poets.org, *Gyroscope Review, Causeway Lit, Linden Avenue Literary Journal, Museum of Americana, RipRap Literary Journal, Carbon Culture Review*, and *Fire and Rain: Ecopoetry of California* by Scarlett Tanager Books, and has been nominated for a Pushcart Prize. Originally from California, he currently lives in Cincinnati, Ohio, where he teaches at Cincinnati State.

www.ingramcontent.com/pod-product-compliance
Lightning Source LLC
LaVergne TN
LVHW041510070426
835507LV00012B/1469